Islands of Wonder
Hawai'i

Text by Chris & Evelyn Cook
with Jan TenBruggencate

Photography by Douglas Peebles

Mutual Publishing

Library of Congress Control Number: 2011936095
ISBN-10: 1-56647-962-2
ISBN-13: 978-1-56647-962-2

First Printing, July 2012
Design by Courtney Young

Mutual Publishing, LLC
1215 Center Street, Suite 210
Honolulu, Hawai'i 96816
Ph: 808-732-1709 / Fax: 808-734-4094
email: info@mutualpublishing.com
www.mutualpublishing.com
Printed in China

CONTENTS

Left: In a land created by violent volcanic eruptions and earthquakes, the cliffs and waterfalls along Hawai'i's North Kohala coast reveal some of the terrain-shaping effects caused by erosion.

Following page: A waterfall plunges from a hanging valley onto a remote beach at the foot of high cliffs on the northern coast of Moloka'i. The island lies between Maui and O'ahu.

INTRODUCTION

**Hawaʻi. Maui. Lānaʻi. Molokaʻi.
Kahoʻolawe. Oʻahu. Kauaʻi. Niʻihau.**

Saying the names of the eight main Hawaiian Islands conjures up an exotic wonderland, far, far away, fragrant with floral scents wafting on gentle tradewinds. The musical island names resonate in the sounds of surf and rustling palms, and fit perfectly a place of rainbows and year-round flowers, neon fish and turquoise waters. And the islands are as rich in natural wonders as their names are melodious.

The largest, Hawaiʻi, hosts a volcano that's been erupting since 1983, offering close-up views of fiery, molten rock. Maui provides unlimited sweeping vistas that redefine the concept of wide-open spaces. Lānai's pineapple plantations have given way to golf courses, but there are still no traffic lights. Old Hawaiʻi's kinship with nature is alive and well on Molokaʻi. Kahoʻolawe is being reborn. Oʻahu, like Honolulu and Waikīkī, reveals a surprising natural serenity at its heart, immune to urban clatter. The loveliness of Kauaʻi inspires breathless awe. Niʻihau's forbidden shores welcome the adventurous.

Each island has something distinctly different to offer. From melted stone hissing steam as it oozes into the ocean, to rock-solid water in the form of ice glittering atop 13,796-foot Mauna Kea, and from the stark moonscape of asphalt-like lava and gray volcanic ash extending for miles in Hawaiʻi Volcanoes National Park, to the countless streams, waterfalls and downpours keeping the lush jungles of its east side moist and green, the Big Island, the largest, possesses the most varied terrain and climate. The two smallest, arid Niʻihau and bone-dry Kahoʻolawe, offer the least variety.

But every island, in it's own unique way, is a treasure chest containing a priceless abundance of nature's wonders: sun-sparkled seas glittering like diamonds, gold sand, silver moonlight, a richness of sunsets, a wealth of waterfalls, and an endless supply of red dirt.

This book is something of a wonder itself, thanks to the talent and skill of veteran photographer Douglas Peebles who has captured in his keen-eyed images the incomparable marvel that is Hawaiʻi.

This page: The flow of molten rock into the sea during the eruption at Kilauea's East Rift Zone creates clouds of acid steam. The lava is instantly solidified upon hitting the water. Some of it shatters into tiny crystals, which wash back ashore to create glistening black sand beaches.

Opposite page: Sea waves create a crust when they wash up onto the molten lava, but the pressure of the flow cracks it open, and the red-orange rock oozes out in fiery lava falls.

VOLCANOES

A river of fiery-orange magma flowing between banks of black lava is a stunning sight, and a window into the primordial process that gave birth to the Hawaiian Islands. The continuing eruption of Kīlauea volcano, which began January 3, 1983, has since added about 570 acres to the island of Hawai'i.

Known as the Big Island, the southernmost of the eight main islands was built by five volcanoes—Kīlauea, Mauna Loa, Hualālai, Mauna Kea and Kohala. The first three are active, Mauna Kea is dormant, and Kohala is said to be extinct. Hualālai, looming over the west-side town of Kailua-Kona, last erupted in 1800 and 1801, and Mauna Loa's last eruption occurred in 1984.

Although none of the other main islands can boast a currently erupting volcano, all were formed by the same process. They are the exposed peaks of a towering undersea range of mountains known as the Hawaiian-Emperor Seamount Chain. The 137 atolls, islets, islands and submerged peaks curve across the North Pacific Ocean for about 1,600 miles. Kure Atoll, the farthest west and north, is the oldest. The Lō'ihi seamount, submerged about 22 miles southeast of the Big Island, is growing and will eventually break the surface to become the newest island.

Hawai'i Volcanoes National Park offers the extraordinary experience of visiting a live volcano. Although Kīlauea has been erupting nearly continuously for more than 28 years, it sometimes takes a rest, so it's a good idea to check for updates before arriving.

A lava fountain at the Puʻu ʻoʻo vent on Kīlauea's East Rift Zone feeds a river of red flowing molten rock.

The lava flow travels miles down the mountainside, sometimes on the surface and sometimes enclosed in lava tubes, to finally reach the sea. The show it puts on is one of nature's most memorable, drawing enraptured audiences from around the globe who view the display with awe.

It's hard to imagine the immense amount of heat (around 2,000 °F) it takes to melt solid rock into flowing streams, but easy to see the startling beauty that results.

Hot lava that hits cool water fractures into tiny particles that wash ashore, creating stunning blacksand beaches like New Beach at Kaimū. Lava buried the famous palm-lined beach here in 1990.

Above: The summit of Hualālai, Hawai'i, peeks above the clouds in the distance. This volcano has not erupted in nearly two centuries, but seismic activity indicates that it is still alive. The views are breath-taking from the 10,023-foot summit.

Opposite page, top photo: The eroding craters at the summit of Hualālai, Hawai'i are clothed in sparse vegetation. Hualālai's last eruptions, in 1800 and 1801, generated lava flows that formed the land upon which Kailua-Kona's airport now stands, seven miles from the town. **Bottom photo:** The caldera of Haleakalā, Maui, features numerous cinder cones that prove secondary volcanic activity. The highest peak on Haleakalā (East Maui Volcano) rises 10,023 feet.

A snowy winter day atop Mauna Kea is considered by astronomers to be one of the best sites in the world for observing the heavens. Several observatories are visible at the summit. Mauna Kea rises nearly 14,000 feet above sea level and has an alpine environment. During cooler global climate conditions, the mountain has supported an ice cap on several occasions.

Hawai'i's state capital, Honolulu, stretches from Punchbowl Crater to Diamond Head. In ancient times, the crater was known as Pūowaina (Hill of Sacrifice) and was a burial ground for Hawaiian royalty, as well as a site where human sacrifices took place. Today, Punchbowl is home to the National Memorial Cemetery of the Pacific, the final resting place for 33,230 members of the United States Armed Forces, many who made the ultimate sacrifice for their country.

This headland jutting into the ocean on the southeastern side of O'ahu is evidence of the island's violent volcanic past. Called Koko Head, it's an ancient eroded tuff cone, formed by an explosive eruption just beneath the ocean's surface. Behind it is another tuff cone, Koko Crater (1,208 feet), with a steep trail to the top, and a great view. Hanauma Bay, which is between the two craters, was also formed by volcanic activity and is a top snorkeling site.

Diamond Head (Lēʻahi), the iconic symbol of Waikīkī, conceals the remains of an almost perfectly round tuff cone within its eroded outer walls. Tuff is a relatively soft rock composed of cemented ash and stone particles created by a sudden explosive eruption in which hot magma comes in contact with water. Geologists believe Diamond Head Crater was formed about 300,000 years ago during a single brief eruption.

LANDFORMS

Long ago, only ocean existed where the Hawaiian Islands now stand. Over millennia, magma burst through the earth's inner mantle and crust and oozed up from beneath the ocean floor into the lower depths of the Pacific, creating a series of undersea volcanoes, which continued erupting, growing towards the surface some 20,000 feet above.

Flowing ever upward and outward, layer after layer of lava built up in the depths, hardening into the foundations upon which successive layers heaped themselves up into seamounts. Year after year, the undersea mountains grew until they finally broke the surface and became the islands called Hawai'i. The same geological forces are in operation today, as the seamount, Lō'ihi, south of the Big Island, continues to expand beneath the ocean's surface, until it, too will one day emerge and become the newest Hawaiian island.

Evidence of ancient seismic upheaval and volcanic activity can be seen in the islands' craggy mountains, sheer cliffs, fluted ridges, volcanic craters, and canyon walls. Additional forces that molded the primordial land forms into their present shapes and configurations also left their mark. Erosion—using rain, wind and wave to accomplish its purpose—carved and polished valleys, gorges, gullies, sea caves and cliff spires, while gradually grinding down mountains, boulders, and coral reefs into the sand for which Hawai'i is famous. An often overlooked force—small but powerful—is the colorful parrot fish. It does its part by utilizing its beak and specialized grinding teeth to devour coral while excreting the waste as sand.

A tour helicopter flies along the steep cliffs and lush valleys of Kaua'i's Nā Pali coast. This spectacular area—formed by volcanic lava flows and massive earthquakes, then sculpted by erosion—is accessible only by air, sea, or foot.

This page: Seismic forces combined with wind and water erosion have created deeply gullied cliffs thousands of feet high on the islands' windward sides. Pictured is an example from Oʻahu's Koʻolau Range. During downpours, the gullies turn into countless long, thin waterfalls—a stunning sight.

Opposite page, top photo: Steep, fluted cliffs, rising to more than 3,000 feet, seem to wrap their arms around Honopū Beach along the dramatic Nā Pali coastline on Kauaʻi. **Bottom photo:** Only a few wisps of cloud are visible on a calm day over Kauaʻi's Kalalau Valley.

Left: Pale yellow-green kukui trees climb up the narrow valleys of Kaua'i's Nā Pali.

Below: The drier habitat of Kaua'i's Waimea Canyon displays the effects of severe and constant erosion.

Opposite page: At Haleakalā, Maui, the dust and cinders are swept into graceful patterns by wind and rain. A narrow ridge ends in a rock spire.

This page: On the beach below Honopū Valley, along Kaua'i's Nā Pali coast, there's a 90-foot natural arch, the tallest in Hawai'i. Honopū means "conch shell." When the wind hits the arch just right, it approximates the sound of a conch being blown.

Opposite page, top photo: Hiking into Waipi'o Valley on the Big Island's northeastern coast is like going back in time. Hawaiians tend taro patches, horses wander freely, and surf leaves white foam on black sand. **Bottom photo:** Magical Waipi'o Valley is hard to get to, and is harder to leave. Waterfalls are abound, including the 1,400- foot-plus Hi'ilawe Falls—the highest in Hawai'i.

Above: Mākua Valley is located on Oʻahu's leeward (southwest) side, extending from the foothills of the Waiʻanae Mountains to the sea. On this side of the island, the climate is drier and hotter than on the moist, windward (northeast) side. The valley holds a special place in Hawaiian hearts. It was here that mankind was created, according to ancient tradition, and there are many "wahi pana" (sacred places) along with valuable cultural and archaeological sites. The U.S. military has been using its 4,000-acre base in the valley for training since the 1930s, which has sometimes created friction with the local populace, but has also so far prevented commercial development.

Left: The Lanipō trail on Oʻahu—a seven-mile round trip—climbs 1,600 feet to the crest of the Koʻolau Range and offers terrific views. The trailhead is next to a Board of Water Supply at the top of Wilhelmina Rise.

ISLANDS & ISLETS

Included within the expansive boundaries of the State of Hawai'i are the eight major islands of Kaua'i, Ni'ihau, O'ahu, Moloka'i, Maui, Lāna'i, Kaho'olawe, and Hawai'i, along with 96 minor islands located off the shores of these main islands. Additionally, ten small islands and atolls make up the Northwestern Hawaiian chain, along with a number of islets within the atolls, some of which appear and disappear from time to time.

The uninhabited Northwestern group includes (from south to north) Nīhoa (about 130 miles northwest of Kaua'i) Necker, French Frigate Shoals, Gardner Pinnacles, Maro Reef, Laysan, Lisianski, Pearl and Hermes Atoll, Midway Atoll, and Kure Atoll. From the Big Island of Hawai'i in the south, to Kure Atoll in the north, the Hawaiian Archipelago consists of about 137 islands, islets and atolls that stretches across some 1,600 miles.

The named islands and islets usually have at least two different appellations, a traditional Hawaiian one and another in English. Mokoli'i, for example—an island in O'ahu's Kāne'ohe Bay– is also known as Chinaman's Hat, presumably because it roughly resembles the headgear worn by Chinese laborers who worked the rice and taro fields a century ago. Its Hawaiian name means "little lizard" and is associated with a number of ancient legends.

Located in the middle of the Pacific Ocean, Hawai'i is the most isolated population center in the world—2,390 miles from California, 3,850 from Japan, 4,900 from China, and 5,280 from the Philippines.

In this aerial view overlooking the windward coast of O'ahu, the 360-foot peak of Rabbit Island can be seen in the foreground. Once a rabbit farm, it's now a bird sanctuary that is closed to the public.

Above: Oʻahu's Kaʻena Point juts westward into Kaʻieʻie Waho Channel. The abundant white foam on the windward side—on the left of the point—compared to the much smaller surf along the leeward shore—is due to the force of the tradewinds (the prevailing winds in the islands), which blow consistently from the northeast.

Each island is wetter on its northeast-facing windward side than on its southwest-facing leeward side because the clouds carried along by the tradewinds stall over the high volcanic mountains that form the spine of each island, dropping most of their moisture before reaching the lee side.

Right: The Hōlei Sea Arch at Hawaiʻi Volcanoes National Park on the Big Island is the result of wave erosion washing away softer rock over a long period of time, leaving an open frame of hard basalt.

Opposite page: Huelo Island stands narrow and tall off Molokaʻi's northern coast, its summit carpeted with a stand of the native loulu palm, which once was a dominant forest tree but is now uncommon.

Above: Hawaiian sailing canoes anchor in front of Mokoli'i, whose unique configuration suggests it is a cinder cone. Actually, it is a sea stack, separated from nearby O'ahu by erosion.

Left: On North Moloka'i, some of the world's highest sea cliffs (3,000 to 4,000 feet) are all that's left of an ancient volcano that collapsed into the sea after a massive earthquake.

Opposite page: In the waters off Maui, Molokini islet attracts snorkelers and divers exploring clear waters and pristine reefs that teem with bright-colored tropical fish and fascinating coral formations. Molokini is the eroded remnant of a tuff cone created by a violent volcanic explosion.

Above: The coral reefs of Kāneʻohe Bay, Oʻahu block ocean swells, thus creating an expanse of flat water that attracts windsurfers, sailors, paddlers, and fishermen. The vast number of colorful fish drawn to the extensive reef system makes for great snorkeling.

Opposite page: Rabbit Island is a seabird sanctuary where tens of thousands of sooty terns, brown noddies, wedge-tailed shearwaters, Bulwers petrels, and red-tailed tropic birds come to breed in spring and summer. Hawaiian Monk seals, an endangered species, haul-out on its beaches. To protect the wildlife, visitors are not allowed, except with a permit from the state Department of Land and Natural Resources. In the 1880s, rabbits were raised on the islet. Over the next 100 years, they multiplied and destroyed so much of the vegetation that it resulted in serious erosion. They were eradicated in the 1990s to protect the seabird nesting sites, as well as the native ecosystem.

RAIN FORESTS & VEGETATION

Moisture-laden clouds carried by northeast tradewinds blowing across the Pacific rip themselves open on the sharp mountain peaks of the Hawaiian Islands, then dump their loads on the north and east sides of the main islands.

That's more of a poetical explanation than a scientifically-sound one, but it contains a simple truth: Hawai'i gets a whole lot of rain.

In one record-setting year, Kaua'i's Mt. Wai'ale'ale received over 600 inches—more than 50 feet. Six miles upland from Hilo, on the east side of the Big Island, the annual average is 300 inches. The north and east sides of O'ahu, Maui, and Moloka'i reliably receive hundreds of inches as well. Only Ni'ihau, Lānai, and Kaho'olawe escape regular, extravagant downpours.

With all that rain, it's only natural that things grow. And with temperatures never falling below freezing except atop the highest peaks, things grow profusely all year around. They grow so much, the islands have convincingly portrayed nearly every rainy, steamy, tropical clime in the world, in the hundreds of feature films lensed in Hawai'i since 1913. The taro patches of Hanalei stood in for the rice paddies of the Viet Nam War. Windward O'ahu passed for the South Pacific jungles of World War II. And Moloka'i masqueraded as the Central American tropics for a dinosaur flick.

The rain doesn't just make things grow. It makes things green, it makes things lush, and it makes them bloom. It also makes waterfalls and rainbows. Without it, Hawai'i wouldn't be Hawai'i.

The rain forest at Hawai'i Volcanoes National Park in Kīlauea, Hawai'i is a complex ecosystem. The most common overstory tree is the 'ōhi'a, which protects a range of species of ferns, vines and shrubs growing below.

Above: Hawai'i's native forests, such as the one along the edge of Alaka'i Swamp on Kaua'i, create superb watersheds, soaking up rains and releasing the moisture slowly into mountain streams, which run even during extended dry weather.

Opposite page: Hapu'u tree fern fronds grow out of fresh lavas at Kīlauea Iki in Hawai'i Volcanoes National Park in Kīlauea, Hawai'i.

Above and right: Red torch ginger and orange heliconia are among hundreds of introduced species growing in Hawai'i. They're beautiful, but non-natives are pushing out endemic plants. Rare species of birds and insects are vanishing from all the islands as noxious weeds and exotic flowers replace the native plants necessary for their survival.

Opposite page: What could be mistaken for colorful moss or lichen growing along the rainy Puna coast on the Big Island is actually seaweed exposed at low tide. Called "limu" in Hawaiian, about 500 varieties grow in the waters surrounding the islands. Nearly 300 are non-native to Hawai'i, and are destroying the state's coral reefs. Scientists have created a machine called the Super Sucker which can remove up to 800 pounds of the harmful weeds in an hour. But there's a big problem: many of the destructive species resemble the native ones, causing confusion and hindering the removal process.

Taro (kalo) provided the main staple of the ancient Hawaiian diet. Prior to Western contact, there were more than 300 distinct varieties, some of which were grown in ponds and others on dry land. Today, it's still an important crop. The taro patches pictured here are in Hanalei, on Kaua'i.

WATERFALLS, RIVERS & STREAMS

Hawai'i's waterfalls are too numerous to count, and come in a variety of shapes and sizes. Many are so remote they're virtually inaccessible, while some of the most beautiful are the easiest to find.

On Kaua'i, Wailuā Falls—an 80-foot, twin cascade—is just outside Līhu'e, not far from the airport. Other Kaua'i favorites include the 800-foot Waipo'o Falls in Kōke'e, and Hanakāpi'ai Falls along the Nā Pali coast.

Kali'uwa'a Falls, also known as Sacred Falls, is located on O'ahu's north shore and can only be viewed from the air. The trail was closed after a rock slide in 1999 killed eight hikers and injured several others. Also on O'ahu is Mānoa Falls, reached by a steep path through a rainforest.

Many of Maui's waterfalls can be found along the road to Hāna. Pu'ohokamoa Falls is a series of falls and pools in the Ka'umahina State Wayside park. Papaw Trail ends at 400-foot Waimoku Falls. There are several other waterfalls along the trail.

On the Big Island, the most accessible falls include Rainbow Falls in Wailuku River State Park near Hilo; 400-ft 'Akaka Falls and its neighbor Hā'ena Falls; and a short drive further, multitiered Uma'uma Falls. A forty-five minute drive beyond that is Waipi'o Valley with its many waterfalls, including 1,400-foot-plus Hi'ilawe Falls.

Rainbow Falls near Hilo drops into a turbulent pool, shaded by giant monstera leaves.

Opposite page: ʻĪao Needle (Kukaʻemoku) is the hard, basaltic core of an ancient volcanic cone that eroded away. It rises 1,200 feet above the ʻĪao Valley near Wailuku, Maui. Hawaiians of old worshipped it as the phallic representation of Kanaloa, the sea god.

Above: Kauaʻi's Wailua Falls drop over a lip of dense basaltic lava, while softer volcanic rock underneath is being eroded away.

Above Near Wailua Falls on Kaua'i, along the banks of the Wailua River, lies Kamokila Village, an authentic replica of a traditional Hawaiian settlement, with grass houses and canoes carved from logs. Open to the public and it's worth a visit.

Right: A Waipi'o Valley waterfall cascades through a rainbow into a plunge pool.

Opposite page: Native shrimps and gobies abound in the small streams of Hawaiian mountains. The gobies have fins fused into small suction cups that help them climb up wet rock faces to get over small waterfalls.

Waterfalls drop into plunge pools on the nearly vertical face of Waimanu Valley in the Big Island's Kohala Mountains. When the rain pours, every groove and crease in the cliff becomes a waterfall.

Plenty of rain—and the abundant mists of 442-foot 'Akaka Falls—support lush vegetation, even on the surrounding cliff faces. To see the falls, on the northeastern Hāmākua Coast of the Big Island, only a short hike is required.

ROCKY COASTS & BEACHES

Since the first Polynesians waded ashore ten centuries ago, the narrow strip of sand and rock where ocean meets land has been both a place for making a living and for having fun. The Hawaiians used sandy beaches for launching their canoes, and rocks made good anchors and strong tools. They used canoes to catch fish to feed their families, as well as for racing and cruising.

Today, the sandy beaches are used to catch tourists who help keep the islands' residents fed. Visitors also come for the rocks, for some of the most spectacular scenery on earth is found along the sheer stone cliffs, solidified lava flows and tumbled boulder fields that make up much of the islands' coastlines.

Hawai'i's volcanic origins explain the wide variety of formations, colors and textures found in rock and sand. Different types of lava are composed of varying combinations of minerals that are broken down and exposed. Wave action, friction, earthquakes and erosion caused by wind and water turn lava flows into boulders, pebbles, and sand.

Kaua'i, Ni'ihau, O'ahu and Moloka'i have the most beaches because these older islands has given nature more time to grind down rock, coral and shell into sand. But only the younger islands of Maui and the Big Island can boast black sand, formed when hot lava hits the ocean. Red, green, gray, and brown sands also occur, but Hawai'i has none of the white-as-sugar variety found in the Caribbean.

Majestic sea cliffs soaring from 3,000 to 4,000 feet, along with four broad, deep valleys, span Moloka'i's north coast from Halawa to the Kalaupapa Peninsula.

Above: Rough ocean swells and big waves crashing against cliffs near Hāna, on Maui's east side, have eaten away at thick layers of lava, leaving behind sea stacks, jagged points, and narrow beaches. Though the Big Island is home to Hawai'i's only currently erupting volcano, Kīlauea, Maui's eastern volcano, Haleakalā, has erupted at least ten times in the past 1,000 years, and a great many more times than that over the past million years. The most recent eruption occurred sometime between 1480 A.D. and 1790. Volcanologists expect more activity from Haleakalā in the future.

Opposite: Lava from the 1800-1801 eruption of Hualālai on the Big Island reached the sea at Ka'ūpūlehu on the west side, about 16 miles north of Kailua-Kona, destroying a Hawaiian village and fishponds, while creating pools that connect to the ocean that provide habitat for juvenile fish and other sea life.

Caressed by foaming surf and embraced by soaring green cliffs and an aquamarine sea, Kaua'i's Honopū Beach is an isolated, serene and lovely place. Visitors must swim in from a boat or nearby Kalalau. Landing boats is not permitted. The swim is rigorous, even in summer when seas are calm.

Above: Tinted by volcanically-produced crystals of olivine, a South Point beach on the Big Island is made mostly of green sand.

Right: Pāpōhaku Beach on Moloka'i is three miles long and 100 yards wide. Sand was formerly mined here for O'ahu's construction industry. Moloka'i is 26 miles from O'ahu.

Once dominant, native hala trees at Lumaha'i Beach, Kaua'i, are now squeezed out by introduced species.

Above: One of east O'ahu's most popular spots, Kailua Beach offers swimming, kayaking, body boarding, wind surfing, and sunbathing—plus shade. Lifeguards are regularly on duty.

Left: In addition to black sand, Maui also has beaches with black pebbles, like this one running under a small arch along the Hāna coastline.

Opposite page: The sand dunes along the beach in the Mo'omomi Preserve on Moloka'i were formed by strong northeast tradewinds.

Following page: Just ten miles from Honolulu on a city bus route, Hanauma Bay—an eroded crater filled with crystal-clear water—is at the top of the "must-see" list for millions of tourists. That may make it seem like a place to avoid, but that would be a mistake. Its easy accessibility, beautiful setting, and huge schools of fish that aren't afraid of people, make this one of the best snorkeling spots in all Hawai'i.

Right: Kīlauea Point, Kaua'i, the site of the northernmost lighthouse in the main Hawaiian Islands, is a seabird nesting site and a national wildlife refuge.

Below: Ask surfers at Hanalei Bay, Kaua'i why he surfs and he'll tell you it's the next best thing to heaven.

Opposite page: A breaking wave forms a perfect tube at Waimea Bay, O'ahu. There's enough power here to splinter a surfboard and bust a surfer's skull against the reef. Yet daredevils ride these monsters for fun.

SUNSET & SUNRISE

Hawaiian skies display epic sunrises and sunsets on a near daily basis. While photographers enjoy recording the show, scientists like to explain it.

Sunlight, they say, is a combination of all the colors in the visual spectrum. The reason that shades of red, orange and yellow predominate in both sunsets and sunrises is because of "Rayleigh scattering" which causes atmospheric dust to break up and nullify the spectrum's blue light. The red/orange/yellow end of the spectrum isn't much affected by dust, so colors at that end—like reddish orange, peachy pink and hibiscus yellow—are the most visible. That's why no one's ever seen a turquoise-blue sunset.

Sunsets are often more vivid than sunrises because there's usually more dust in the lower atmosphere at the end of the day than at the beginning. During the day, the sun heats the surface of the earth, lowering the relative humidity and increasing wind speed and turbulence, which lifts dust into the air. Volcanic dust from the Big Island's eruption enhances the colors.

Sunsets and sunrises over the ocean are the most dramatic. At Kīlauea Point Lighthouse on Kaua'i, the sun can be seen rising in the east over the Pacific at dawn, then sinking below the Pacific's western horizon at sundown.

Lava rocks and palm fronds punctuate a spectacular sunset at Poipu on Kaua'i. Volcanic dust from the Big Island, 200 miles away, intensifies the color.

Right: 'Alau Island off Hāna stands in an orange sea at sunrise.

Below: A sunrise at Punalu'u, on northeast O'ahu, silhouettes swaying coconut palms. The clouds will become great puffs of white floating across the blue sky as soon as the sun comes up.

Opposite page: Kaua'i's Kalalau Beach at sunset, looking southwest along Nā Pali. To get to this vantage point without the aid of an aircraft requires a long hike, strenuous swim, or boat ride. There is no road.

Following page: Sunset on the Kohala Coast along the northwest shore of the Big Island, an area of premier golf courses and luxury resorts.